Wheelchair Field Events

by James R. Little, Ph.D.

Content Consultant

Barry M. Ewing
Chairman
Wheelchair Sports, USA

RiverFront Books

An imprint of Franklin Watts
A Division of Grolier Publishing
New York London Hong Kong Sydney
Danbury, Connecticut

RiverFront Books
http://publishing.grolier.com

Printed in the United States of America.

Library of Congress Cataloging-in-Publication Data
Little, James R.
    Wheelchair field events / by James R. Little.
        p. cm. -- (Wheelchair sports)
    Includes bibliographical references (p. 45) and index.
    Summary: Introduces wheelchair field events, relates the history of these activities for the physically handicapped, and discusses the rules, equipment, and training needed to participate safely.
    ISBN 1-56065-617-4
    1. Wheelchair track-athletics--Juvenile literature.
[1. Wheelchair track and field. 2. Sports for the physically handicapped.
3. Physically handicapped.] I. Title. II. Series.
GV1060.93.L58   1998   97-19256
796.42--DC21   CIP
                                               AC

Editorial Credits
Editor, Greg Linder; cover design and logo, Timothy Halldin; photo research, Michelle L. Norstad
Photo Credits
Sports 'N Spokes/Paralyzed Veterans of America, cover, 6, 8, 11, 13, 28, 32, 44; Curt Beamer, 4, 7, 12, 19, 22, 36, 39, 40-41; Curt Beamer and Delfina Colby, 26; Delfina Colby, 25, 31, 34
Tom Pantages, 16, 20
Unicorn Stock/Jean Higgins, 15
Special thanks to *Sports 'N Spokes*/PVA Publications and Wheelchair Sports, USA, for their assistance.

Table of Contents

Chapter 1
Field Events

W heelchair field events include the shot put, the discus, the javelin, and the club throw. These field events are sports contests performed by wheelchair athletes. An athlete is a person who is trained for a sport or a game. A wheelchair athlete uses a wheelchair when playing the sport or game.

Wheelchair athletes have spinal cord injuries or similar problems. A spinal cord injury is damage to the spinal cord. This part of the body controls nerves and muscles. Because wheelchair athletes cannot stand or walk, they perform their events while seated.

Wheelchair field athletes perform their events while seated.

The club looks like a bowling pin.

Shot-putters try to push a heavy metal ball through the air. Discus throwers sail a wooden disc that looks like a flying saucer. Javelin throwers toss a metal stick with a pointed tip. Club throwers throw an object that looks like a bowling pin. The winner of each event is the wheelchair athlete who sends each object the farthest distance.

Javelin throwers toss a pointed metal stick.

Chapter 2
History

Field events are among the oldest known sports events. They were part of the early Olympic Games, which began more than 2,700 years ago. The first Olympics were held on the fields of Olympia in Greece. Only Greek athletes competed in the games. Today's Olympic Games are sports contests among athletes from many nations.

Wheelchair Sports

Before World War II (1939-1945), there were no wheelchair sports leagues. Near the end of the war, wounded soldiers filled hospitals in many countries. Doctors started rehabilitation programs for these soldiers. Rehabilitation means helping people recover their health or abilities. Doctors

Field events are among the oldest known sports events.

thought patients in wheelchairs could strengthen their arms and upper bodies by playing sports.

Wheelchair sports programs began in Canada, Great Britain, and the United States during the 1940s. The rules of some sports were changed so that people in wheelchairs could play. For most sports, only a few rules were changed.

Sir Ludwig Guttmann was the director of the Stoke Mandeville Hospital in England. In 1948, Guttmann put together the first wheelchair games. The games took place in England a few weeks after the 1948 London Olympics. Twenty-six wheelchair athletes from Great Britain competed. Three of them were women. The only sport they competed in was archery.

In 1952, Guttmann created the first international wheelchair games. International means including people from more than one country. The 1952 games featured the shot put, the javelin, and the club throw. Athletes from

The shotput was one event featured at the 1952 international wheelchair games.

The first wheelchair athletes brought wheelchair sports to the attention of the world.

Great Britain competed against athletes from the Netherlands. These athletes brought wheelchair sports to the attention of the world.

National wheelchair games began in the United States and Canada in 1957. National means including people from one nation. These national games take place every year.

The Paralympics
In 1960, the international wheelchair games

Athletes from many countries compete at the Paralympic Games.

became known as the Paralympic Games. The Paralympics are contests like the Olympics, but the athletes are people with disabilities. A person with disabilities is someone who has a permanent illness, injury, or birth defect. A permanent disability is a disability that cannot be fixed or cured.

The Olympics and the Paralympics are always held during the same year. In fact, they both take place in the same city. The 1960 Paralympics were held in Rome, Italy, shortly after the Rome Olympics. The Paralympics drew 400 athletes from 23 countries. The United States and Canada have sent wheelchair athletes to every Paralympics since 1960.

The Olympics and the Paralympics are held every four years. The 1996 Paralympic Games were held in Atlanta, Georgia. In 1996, 3,500 athletes from 120 countries came to compete. That year, the Paralympics were the second-largest sports event in the world. Only the 1996 Olympic Games drew more athletes.

The 1996 Paralympic Games were the second-largest sports event of the year.

Chapter 3
Individual Events

Field athletes throw the javelin, the discus, and the club from within a circle. The shot put is pushed into the air from the same circle. This circle is called the throwing circle. The throwing circle is seven feet (about two meters) across.

The athletes aim for the throwing area. The throwing area is the area in which the thrown object must land. If the object lands outside of the throwing area, it is out of bounds.

Able-bodied athletes can walk, spin, or run across the throwing circle. This adds force to their throws. Wheelchair athletes must remain seated in a chair. They can turn their bodies from side to side. But sitting in the chair prevents them from turning more than about

Athletes throw the javelin from within a throwing circle.

halfway around. Their wheelchairs and their bodies must remain inside the throwing circle during the event.

Top Olympic athletes have performed field events while sitting in a chair. They do about as well as top wheelchair athletes. Throwing or pushing from a chair takes strength and practice.

The Shot Put

The shot is a heavy, round object made of hard metal. The official shot for wheelchair sports must weigh eight pounds, 13 ounces (four kilograms). It is about the size of a softball.

The shot rests on the athlete's fingers. It is supported by the thumb. The shot-putter must hold the shot above the shoulder, but under the ear. The athlete uses the shoulder, arm, and wrist to push the shot toward the throwing area. This pushing motion is called putting.

The athlete pushes the shot toward the throwing area.

The shot leaves a mark when it hits the ground. Officials measure the distance between the mark and the throwing circle. The winning athlete is the one who pushes the shot the farthest distance. A top wheelchair shot-putter can put the shot as far as 39 feet (11.7 meters).

The shot must be pushed, not thrown. If an athlete throws the shot, the throw is disqualified. Disqualified means not allowed. The athlete's throw is not measured or scored.

The Discus

The discus looks like two Frisbees pressed together. The official discus for wheelchair sports is made of wood and has a metal rim. It weighs two pounds, three ounces (one kilogram). A good athlete throws the discus so it sails steadily through the air. If it tips or wobbles, it will not go very far.

The discus should sail steadily through the air.

The discus rests on the palm of the hand. The ends of the fingers extend over the metal rim. During the throw, the athlete turns the hand so the palm faces down. The weight of the discus holds it against the athlete's fingers.

The discus leaves a mark when it hits the ground. Officials measure the distance between the mark and the throwing circle. The winning athlete is the one who throws the discus the farthest. Top wheelchair throwers have thrown the discus about 44 feet (13.2 meters).

The wheelchair athlete must remain seated until the discus has been thrown. A throw is disqualified if the athlete rises from the chair.

The Javelin

The javelin looks like a spear made of lightweight metal. Its pointed tip allows it to stick in the ground when it lands. For wheelchair sports, the javelin must weigh one pound, seven

The javelin should stick in the ground when it lands.

ounces (644 grams). It must be seven feet, eight inches (2.3 meters) long.

The javelin has a cord grip in the middle. The cord grip is a small rope wrapped tightly around the javelin. It helps the athlete hold onto the javelin. During a throw, the cord grip rests in the palm of an athlete's hand. The athlete throws the javelin overhand, just as a baseball pitcher throws a baseball.

The tip of the javelin must stick in the ground when it lands. Officials measure the distance between the javelin and the throwing circle. The winning athlete is the one who throws it the farthest. Wheelchair javelin throwers have thrown the javelin as far as 118 feet (35.4 meters).

If the javelin does not stick in the ground, the throw is disqualified. Many athletes can throw the javelin a great distance, but making it stick takes practice.

The javelin has a cord grip in the middle.

The Club Throw

The club is 15 inches (39 centimeters) long. It weighs less than a pound (less than one-half kilogram). The club looks like a thin bowling pin. Athletes who cannot hold things with their finger and hand muscles compete in the club throw.

The club is pressed firmly between two fingers. Some athletes coat the club with a jelly-like substance. The sticky substance helps the club stay in the athlete's hand. During a throw, the weight of the club pulls it into the air.

The club leaves a mark when it hits the ground. Officials measure the distance between the mark and the throwing circle. Wheelchair club throwers have thrown the club as far as 80 feet (24 meters).

The club must land in the throwing area. If it does not, the throw is disqualified.

The club is pressed firmly between two fingers.

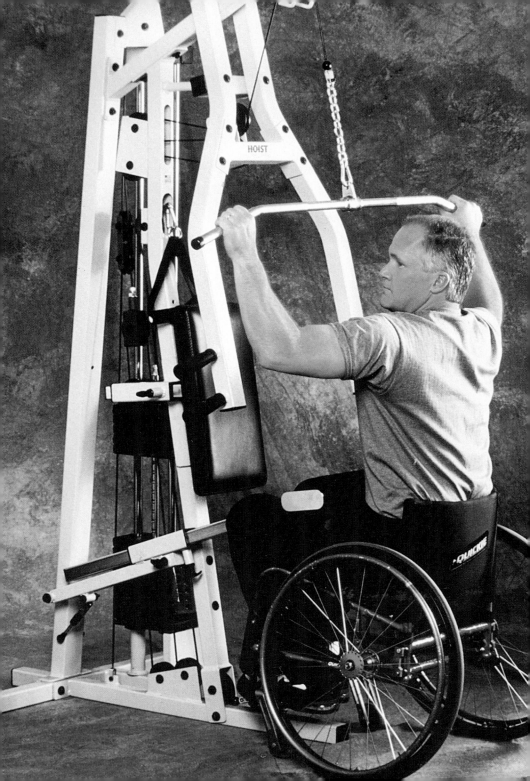

Chapter 4
The Athletes

Many wheelchair field athletes are paraplegics. A paraplegic is a person who has little or no ability to move the lower part of the body. A paraplegic athlete works hard to strengthen the upper half of the body.

Training
Wheelchair field athletes train all year. They practice their events to develop proper throwing or pushing technique. Technique is a style or way of doing something. The athletes do stretching and body turning exercises. They lift weights to strengthen their arm and upper body muscles.

Many field athletes also play wheelchair tennis or wheelchair basketball. These sports help them stay in good condition.

Wheelchair athletes may lift weights to strengthen arm and upper body muscles.

Who Can Enter?

A field athlete must have a permanent disability in one or both legs. People with temporary disabilities are not allowed to enter wheelchair field events.

Wheelchair field athletes are divided into eight classes. Those in class F1 are the most severely disabled. They are quadriplegics. A quadriplegic is a person who has limited ability to move the upper and lower parts of the body. A quadriplegic cannot use hand and finger muscles to hold onto things.

Athletes in class F8 are the least disabled. These paraplegics have some control over their leg and foot muscles. However, they cannot walk, run, or jump without difficulty. They can sit without support, and their upper bodies are quite strong.

People called classifiers decide which athletes belong in each class. Classifiers are

Some wheelchair field athletes play basketball to stay in good condition.

specially trained doctors who work with disabled athletes.

Wheelchair field athletes in each class compete against one another. Men compete against men, and women compete against women. Young athletes are divided into five age groups. Athletes as young as six years old compete against others in their age group.

In field events, men compete against men, and women compete against women.

Chapter 5

Equipment and Safety

Before the 1992 Paralympics in Barcelona, Spain, field athletes had to throw from sports wheelchairs. Then the rule changed. Athletes were allowed to throw from any seat no higher than 2 feet, 6 inches (75 centimeters) off the ground.

Athletes, coaches, and wheelchair builders started making customized throwing chairs. A customized chair is a wheelchair built to fit the size and shape of its user.

Most throwing chairs have rear wheels like bicycle tires. But during a field event, the wheels are popped off. Without wheels, the chair is like a stool. Most chairs have a short back and an armrest on each side.

During a field event, a throwing chair's wheels are popped off.

The throwing chair must be strong and stable. But it should be small and light enough to be taken in a car, a van, or an airplane. Modern throwing chairs weigh between 25 and 50 pounds (11 and 23 kilograms).

Seat Belts and Leg Straps

Athletes use seat belts to keep them from falling out of the chairs. The belts also help stop forward motion at the end of a throw. They are like the seat belts used in cars.

Leg straps help keep an athlete's feet from touching the ground. A throw is disqualified if any part of the athlete touches the ground during the throw.

Tie-Down Straps and Anchor Pins

The athlete's throwing chair must be anchored to the ground before each field event. This is done so the chair does not move or slip while the

Throwing chairs are anchored to the ground.

athlete performs. Anchoring a chair is much like tying down the corners of a camping tent.

Most athletes use nylon tie-down straps. A strap has a hook on each end. A clamp in the middle keeps the strap tight. The hook on one end of the strap is fastened to a corner of the wheelchair. The hook on the other end of the strap is connected to a metal pin. The metal pin is pounded into the ground. All four corners of the chair are anchored in this way. The metal pins are called anchor pins.

Safety

Throwing chairs are built to be safe. They are made of lightweight but strong metal. Any sharp edges or metal bolts are covered with soft padding. The padding protects the athlete from being hurt by the throwing chair. Metal pieces are welded together to make them stronger. Welding is heating pieces of metal until they are soft enough to be connected.

For the wheelchair field athlete, safety means staying strong and healthy. It means keeping the throwing chairs in good working

Top wheelchair athletes have a chance to set new world records.

condition. And it means handling the javelin, discus, shot put, or club safely.

Athletes must be aware of other people during field events. A wild throw could hurt onlookers, other athletes, or officials.

Like other athletes, wheelchair athletes compete for fun and for a challenge. They know if they work hard, they can improve their performance. The best wheelchair field athletes have a chance to set new world records.

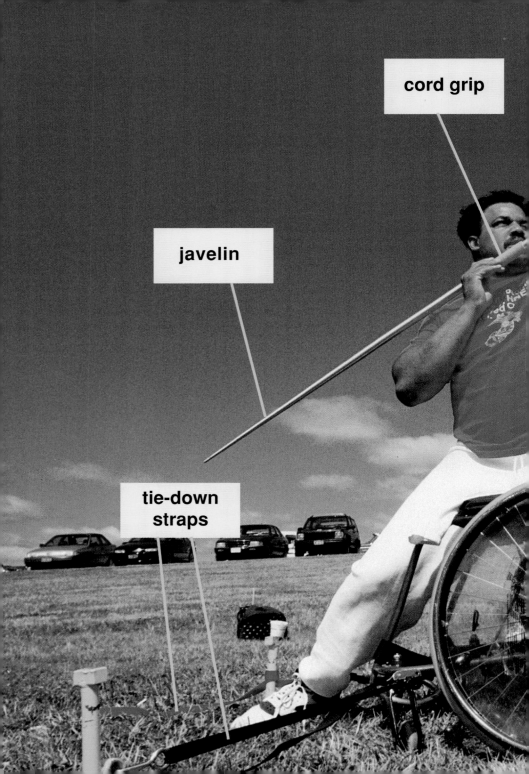

cord grip

javelin

tie-down
straps

wheel

anchor pins

Words to Know

anchor pin (ANG-kur PIN)—a metal pin used to anchor wheelchairs

classifier (KLASS-uh-fye-ur)—a specially trained doctor who works with disabled athletes

cord grip (KORD GRIP)—a small rope wrapped tightly around a javelin

disqualified (diss-KWOL-uh-fyed)—not allowed

Olympic Games (oh-LIM-pik GAMES)—sports contests between athletes from many nations

Paralympic Games (pa-ruh-LIM-pik GAMES)—sports contests like the Olympic Games for athletes with disabilities

paraplegic (pa-ruh-PLEE-jik)—a person who has little or no ability to move the lower part of the body

permanent disability (PUR-muh-nuhnt diss-uh-BIL-uh-tee)—a disability that cannot be fixed or cured

person with disabilities (PUR-suhn WITH diss-uh-BIL-i-teez)—someone who has a permanent illness, injury, or birth defect

putting (PUT-ing)—the pushing motion used by shot-putters

quadriplegic (kwahd-ruh-PLEE-jik)—a person who has limited ability to move the upper and lower parts of the body; a quadriplegic cannot use hand and finger muscles to hold onto things

rehabilitation (ree-huh-bil-uh-TAY-shun)—helping people recover their health or abilities

spinal cord injury (SPYE-nul KORD IN-juh-ree)—damage to the part of the body that controls nerves and muscles

technique (tek-NEEK)—a style or way of doing something

throwing area (THROH-ing AIR-ee-uh)—the area in which a thrown or pushed object must land

throwing circle (THROH-ing SUR-kuhl)—the circle used by athletes during field events

To Learn More

Rosenthal, Bert. *Track and Field: How to Play the All-Star Way.* Austin, Tex.: Raintree Steck-Vaughn, 1994.

Savitz, Harriet May. *Wheelchair Champions.* New York: Crowell, 1978.

Smale, David. *Track and Field.* Mankato, Minn.: Smart Apple Media, 1995.

Weisman, Marilee and Jan Godfrey. *So Get on with It: A Celebration of Wheelchair Sports.* Toronto: Doubleday Canada, 1976.

You can learn more about wheelchair track and field events in *Sports 'N Spokes* magazine.

Useful Addresses

Wheelchair Sports USA
3595 East Fountain Boulevard
Colorado Springs, CO 80910

Canadian Wheelchair Sports Association
1600 James Naismith Drive
 Gloucester, ON K1B 5N4
Canada

Mexican Wheelchair Sport Program
Federacion Mexicana de Deportes Sobre Silla
   de Ruedas y Rehabilitados AC
Edificio Codeme Cubiculo 306
Puerta 9 CD Deportiva
Mexico 08010 DF

Internet Sites

British Wheelchair Athletics Association
http://info.lut.ac.uk/research/paad/Wheelpower/
  BWSF/Sports/Athletics-Field/bwaa.html

Canadian Wheelchair Sports Association
http://indie.ca:80/cwsa/history.html

International Paralympic Committee
http://info.lboro.ac.uk/research/paad/ipc/ipc.html

University of Illinois Wheelchair Sports
http://www.als.uiuc.edu/dres/wc-sports

Index